How to Grow Kids

From the
Heart of

Andy

Book One

Wendy Iscove, BSc.N., M. A.

Illustrations by Dax Schaffer

Archway Publishing books may be ordered through booksellers or by contacting:

Archway Publishing
1663 Liberty Drive
Bloomington, IN 47403
www.archwaypublishing.com
1 (888) 242-5904

Because of the dynamic nature of the Internet, any web addresses or links contained in this book may have changed since publication and may no longer be valid. The views expressed in this work are solely those of the author and do not necessarily reflect the views of the publisher, and the publisher hereby disclaims any responsibility for them.

Any people depicted in stock imagery provided by Thinkstock are models, and such images are being used for illustrative purposes only.
Certain stock imagery © Thinkstock.

ISBN: 978-1-4808-4409-4 (sc)
ISBN: 978-1-4808-4410-0 (e)

Library of Congress Control Number: 2017903059

Print information available on the last page.

Archway Publishing rev. date: 5/10/2017

Andy shows his parents what he needs to…

Grow Strong Socially and Emotionally

How To Grow Kids - From the Heart of Andy

You love your kids, but sometimes, just can't figure out what they need.

Andy speaks in a clear and direct way to help us understand those needs, and suggests ways to meet those needs.

He doesn't have all the answers, but has learned some things along the way, and hopes to share them with you.

Author – Wendy Iscove BSc.N, M.A.

Illustrations and Layouts – Dax Schaffer B.A.

Additional Design/Layouts – Larry Williamson R.G.D.

Acknowledgments…

I want to thank my parents, Ken and Beryl Maltby,
and my brother David, for providing me with a
remarkable foundation for knowing love.

And to David, Adam, and Emily….
You taught me that above all else,
children are to be loved and respected.

Finally, I'd like to thank God for showing up every
morning, upon request, to work with me.

This book is to be shared with all boys and girls, their parents,
grandparents, and all caregivers.
Gender is used interchangeably throughout the book.

On the back of most pages, you'll find the word, "More"…..
Below is information intended to flush-out or more fully expand the
ideas on the front of the page.

Chapter

Based on a true story...

Introduction

Before we get started,
here are 4 important things
you need to know:

1. You are my
best teacher.

"I learn
everything
from you."

More.........

A truth: You know in your heart, that no one will love me, take care of me, or teach me the way you will. You are my world. You bring the world to me, and teach me how "to be," in that world. I look to you as my first and best teacher.

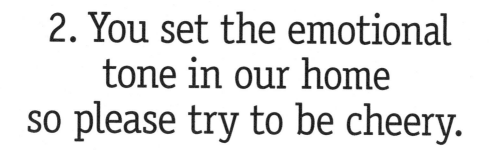

2. You set the emotional
tone in our home
so please try to be cheery.

More………

I look to you, everyday, to create a happy and encouraging feeling in our home. I feel safe when I'm inside a happy home and learn to trust that the world outside, for the most part, can be a happy place, too. When there are "big feelings" floating around our family or fighting of any kind, I need YOU to bring our home, back into balance.

I watch and take cues from your body and face; my responses will match your responses. For example, if you are soured by a rainy or snowy day, I will probably feel the same. However, if you see the rain as an opportunity for the flowers and grass to have a drink and for me to have fun splashing in some puddles, then I can see the magic in rainfall, as well.

3. Try to always come from a place of love.

More.......

When I have just done something that makes you angry, try your best to take the "high road," by coming from a place of love or instruction. This means you're being asked to calm yourself enough to be able to see most accidents or mistakes I make, as learning opportunities for me or teaching moments for you.

Ask yourself,
"How can I best respond?"
OR
"What do I want her to know?"

More..........

I look to you for everything, for most of the support, in my life. I see myself through your eyes; that is, I see my own reflection from you, my parent. So I am who you say I am. This suggests a pretty big responsibility for you because what you are reflecting is growing my "sense of myself."

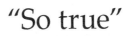

"So true"

If you say I'm a good boy,
who has made a mistake,
but tries sooo hard...

...then, that is who I am.

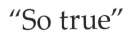

"So true"

Read ahead and see…

What I Need
and
How You Can Help Me

"Read on"

To Feel Safe and Calm

"Read on"

I Need To Feel Safe.

When we're away from home,
keep me close to you.

Don't let me get lost.

More.........

I need to know that you or the people taking care of me will keep me safe and protected. Knowing this helps me to build trust with you, and those around me.

When I feel safe, I feel calm inside. When I feel calm, I have the brain power that I need to explore and learn new skills.

When I don't feel safe, I spend most of my brain power trying to calm myself down. But then, I have very little energy left to put toward learning new things.

The bottom line is this: I do my best learning, when I feel safe and calm inside.

More..........

It really is important for you to keep your eyes on me when we're at the park or a play-space. It lets me know that you are there to help me if I should fall or, in some way, hurt myself. Plus… I like to show you how well I'm learning new skills like going down the slide or swinging or climbing.

I like you to spend a good
"quantity" of time with me,
not just "quality" time.

I feel calm and safe inside
when I know you're close-by.

More..........

Staying close to me really is important, to me. The quantity of time, as well as the quality of time spent with me, DOES MATTER.
This physical closeness comforts me and helps me to feel safe.
When I feel calm, I can be strong. Feeling strong helps me grow my "sense of myself."

When you're able to stop your work long enough to play with me, this tells me that you are aware of my need to be close to you and to laugh and share time with you. There are many ways we can be close during the day: take me on errands, stop at the park for a quick playtime, let me help you set the table for dinner or cook with you. At the same time, while we're doing those fun things, I'm watching how you speak to people around us; and so, I'm learning new language and social skills from you, as well.

If you work outside our home, I know you'll find someone to care for me who will keep me safe and happy.

Make our home safe to play inside...

yes

no

More………

I know you'll keep me safe by installing safety locks on cupboards and cabinets. As well, I need some simple, yet safe, things to play with, inside and outside our home. These playthings help me to exercise my body and my brain. You don't need to spend a lot of money on these things; some of the best toys are right here, in our home. I can use them in imaginative ways.

For example:

I can use those big-box cartons, from your shopping, as tunnels for inside and outside play.

I can line up shoe-boxes to create a balance beam.

I can gather old toys or jewelry and play "Store."

I can fill old milk containers with sand to use as bowling pins.

I can hide kitchen tools around the house for "Hide and Seek."

...and safe...

...to play outside.

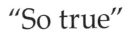

"So true"

Please try to be careful with what
I watch and hear.

Some pictures and sounds are
too scary for me.

More………….

Please, try to watch movies, TV shows, videogames, listen to music and material from the internet, before I see or hear them. Many pictures and sounds are just too scary for me. I can't make meaning of them or understand them because my understanding is not as big as yours, yet.

Once I see a scary image, I can't "un-see" it.

Once I hear a scary sound, I can't "un-hear" it.

Please be careful about what you put in front of me.

At the beginning, stand up for me when I can't do it for myself.

I'll eventually learn how to solve problems on my own.

More.........

I need to know I can count on you, to help me, when I'm in a fight with someone. Help me learn how to figure my way through it, until I can do it for myself. I need to know you'll treat both of us fairly, while helping us work through the problem. I learn by watching what you SAY and DO.

Suggestions for How to Help:

1. You see me as I'm being pushed or hit. You won't let anyone hurt me so, you try to stay calm, but firm, as you say to the other child, "We don't hit or shove. I can't let you hit my son. What's going on here? Or..... Let's talk about this!"

2. Another time, you see me pushing or hitting another child. You stay calm, but firm, as you say to me, "We don't hit or shove. I would not let her hit you and I cannot let you hit her. Let's talk about what happened." This shows me that you will treat everyone in the same and fair manner.

3. Another time, I am in a fight and you don't see what happened. Stay calm, but firm, as you say, "We don't hit. I didn't see what happened, but I can't let you both hurt each other. Let's talk about what happened." Again, everyone is treated in the same and fair manner.

4. When we're fighting over play equipment, you say, plainly, "At the park, we all share. We all take turns."

To Have Order and Boundaries

"Read on"

I Need Order and Boundaries
These make me feel safe
because they tell me:
What I can do and what I can't do

OR

What I can have and
what I can't have.

More.........

I feel calm and safe when I see these two things in our home:

1. Order
When you keep our home clean and organized, this makes me happy.

This is why:

When my toys are in their own bins or boxes, I can see what I have to play with. When I know that my toys are in the same place, everyday, I can go right to them instead of spending time, looking for them.
And, I like it when our home looks and smells clean, too.

2. Boundaries
It's a good idea when all of us, at home, agree to behave or act a certain way; these agreements help us know what is expected of us.

Here are few things to think about:

- We can *create* these agreements by all of us talking about them, together.

- *Explain* to us why we have certain agreements.

- *Practise* them with us, so we can learn how to do them.

Examples of agreements:
We will take care of our toys.
We will help with a job, when asked.

This is how I learn about order and boundaries:

Teach me......Don't punish me!

Show me......

What to do!   Instead of   What not to do!

More........

When I do something wrong, try to always come from a place of LOVE. Try to **teach me** instead of **punish me.** When you scold me or tell me WHAT NOT TO DO, that usually stops my actions for that one time, only. Instead, when you teach me WHAT TO DO, this shows me the best (appropriate) action to take, at this time. This guidance helps me to feel safe, because it reminds me that I'm living in a home where everyone knows how to behave, and what is expected of them. Don't forget to explain to me WHY you want me to act a certain way.

Example:

Sadly and without thinking, I try to squash snails on the sidewalk. Stop me and say, "These are living things on the planet, just like you and me. Let's lift them up and put them back in the garden where they belong." This tells me WHAT is expected of me or what is the appropriate way to behave. Finally, you could say, "We take care of all living creatures." This tells me WHY I should behave that way.

If I make a mistake, tell me that
WHAT I DID was NOT okay,

but that you still love me.

More.............

When you put a label on me, such as a "bad girl" or a "bad boy," this is what I hear in my heart, "I am bad and you don't love me, anymore." These words make me feel ashamed of myself and bad about myself. When I feel shame, I'm so upset, I can't even hear you, as you talk to me. I can't learn when I feel so badly about myself. I just get stuck in the big, bad feelings, about myself.

Suggestion:

It would really help me if you said something like this, "What you DID, or your BEHAVIOR, was NOT OK... but, I still LOVE YOU."

More.........

It is important that I learn to be kind to others. Part of that learning is to recognize that my own actions have consequences. First, I must see and understand how those actions affect those around me. Please point this out to me, when you see it happening.

Show me how I can
fix a mistake to make things
better.

" I'm sorry."

More.........

I need to know that I "can do" something to try and fix a problem I've created. One thing I can do is to say, "I am sorry for what I did." It helps me feel good about myself, and powerful, to know that I can change certain things or try to make them "right" again. This shows me that life can often return to "normal," or to a calm state, once again.

When you get angry at me or others, don't get too crazy. That scares me!

More..............

When you scream and rage at me, or someone else, this frightens me. You kind of look like a fire-breathing dragon, that needs a "time out." (Just kidding). But, I do need to know that the dragon will go away soon, and that you'll come back to keep our home and me safe.

Some things to think about:

1. It's OK to feel angry at me; don't try to hide your anger or bottle it up until you explode. You don't need to be a "perfect" parent.

2. It's WHAT you DO with that anger, that is important. Don't ever hit me.

3. Show me ways you bring your own anger under control.

Suggestions:

1. Say, "I am really angry right now about...(whatever just happened), so I'm going to take some time out to calm myself down and think about it."

or

2. Say, "I am feeling very upset right now. So I'm going to give myself a "time out" to calm myself down, then we can talk about what happened. I'm going to sit in my favorite chair and play some soothing music."

or

3. Say, "I feel frustrated with what you just did, so I'm going to calm myself first, before we talk. I'll take some deep breaths and count to 10."

Again, I learn by watching what you SAY and DO. I will react as you react.

If you need to correct me, please speak to me alone.
This helps me "save face"
with my friends.

More……..

How I look to my friends (part of my self-image) is really, really
important to me. It hurts so much when you scold me in front of them.
I feel ashamed and just all bad inside. I always like to look good to them.
If I've done something wrong, please ask me to step away with you,
while you speak to me, on my own. That feels soooo much better.

I need to know I can't have everything I want.

More……..

Boy! Is this a hard lesson! I know, I know ……. I will learn it eventually!

Please be reliable. Keep your word. When you say you're going to do something....DO IT!

More……..

Doing what you say you're going to do helps to build trust between us.

Be consistent by picking me up on time.

More……..

When your actions show me that I can count on you to do the same things, most of the time (be consistent and reliable), I learn to trust you.

Please be consistent.

This lets me know that I can count on the same things happening every day, at about the same time.

Routines and schedules are ways to be consistent.

I feel safe when we can use these things at home.

More………..

Guys….You don't have to be the only keepers of the schedules!

If you could post these suggested picture schedules (see next pages) around the house, I can go to them, to see what's coming next, in my day. These schedules are simply pictures that show me WHAT happens and WHEN it happens, around our home. I feel strong and capable when I know what is happening, as well. It also teaches me how to be independent, when you say to me, "It's time for bed.
Why don't you go and look at your schedule to see what you have to do, to get ready for bed."

Morning Routine

Only Suggestions
(Post this in my room)

Wake up

Breakfast

Play hard outside

Bathroom jobs:
face, teeth & hair

Get dressed

Mid-morning snack

Afternoon Routine

(Post on refrigerator)

Lunch

Quiet time

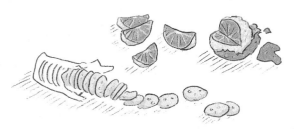

Snack

More play

Evening Routine

(Post in my room or den)

Dinner

Bath & teeth

Reading

Time for bed

Red Flag!

Don't forget to let me know what is coming next in my day.

Give me a five minute warning of a change that is about to happen.

This warning is called a "transition."

More.........

When you pull me away from my playing, without giving me a warning, it's like yanking me awake, from a deep sleep.

It would help me to have a couple of minutes to prepare my feelings, for the change that is coming. This time allows me to say goodbye to one activity before I go on to the next activity. When you give me this warning, it shows me you respect me; you're telling me that you understand I need time to switch gears.

You could say, "I know it's hard to leave that game, so I'm giving you a 5-minute warning to end your playing."

To Give Love
and Feel Love

"Read on"

I Need To Know I Am Loved
And That I Belong

First of all, I know
I am not you –

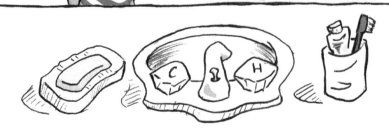

I am me, I am a child.
I am separate from you.

"So true"

I need you to love me for who I am.

Say, "We like you the way you are!"

More……..

I need to know I am loved and that you love me, not for what I do or how I look, but simply because I am alive and I'm your son or daughter. This shows me that you think I'm important to you, which helps me feel happy and strong inside.

I need you to cuddle me.

More..........

When you cuddle me, or toss me, or kiss and gently touch me....this helps my brain grow and work better.

It's almost as important as food to me.

Not to mention, when I cuddle you back, I think you like it, too.

I need to know I make you happy.

More………..

When you play with me and spend time with me, it shows me that you like to be with me. When I see that I can make you smile or make you happy, I feel good about that; this makes me feel strong and powerful inside. Feeling strong inside helps me grow my "sense of myself."

Take the time to explain things to me and talk with me.

More……..

I know that I need to explore many things on my own; however, I also need you to explain a lot about the world, to me. Please, answer my questions, the WHAT, WHY, WHERE, WHEN, and WHO questions, that will help me understand the world.

Caution: Don't over-explain things to me. You can tell by my face when I'm in overload or you've given me "too much information." So, keep it short and simple.

Please listen when I speak to you
....and please look at my face.

More.........

Don't forget to get down to my level, sometimes, when we talk together. When you stop, look at me, and give me your attention, you're showing me that you respect me and my needs.

Show me I belong to a family.

More……..

I am happy to know I am part of a family group. However big or small it is, that group can include aunts, uncles, cousins, close neighbors or friends. I feel happy and safe when I am in such a group, because it lets me know that there are other people around me, or in my world, who could take care of me, if I needed that.

Living with family and close friends helps me see how other people live; it shows me what we share in common. Knowing that I belong to this family or community group helps me feel safe and happy.

PHEW! – Growing Kids is a lot of work!

But it can be fun for both of us.

If you could practise some of
these suggestions,
it would show me
that you respect me.

When you love and
respect me....
I learn to love and
respect you.

Don't forget,
you're my best teacher.
I learn everything from YOU!